TORN

Shahanaz M Meera

pencil

ISBN 978-93-5458-418-3

Published in India 2021 by Pencil

A brand of
One Point Six Technologies Pvt. Ltd.
123, Building J2, Shram Seva Premises,
Wadala Truck Terminal, Wadala (E)
Mumbai 400037, Maharashtra, INDIA
E connect@thepencilapp.com
W www.thepencilapp.com

Author biography

Shahanaz M Meera is a poet who has been writing various genres of poems since 2017. A Software Engineer at the moment, writing poems turned out to be a passion upon which she is trying to succeed. She has been writing on All-Poetry and on other platforms through which she is trying to make an impact.

CONTENTS

Don't Need This Road to Extend 7

Wave of My Thoughts 8

You Never Talked to Me Then 9

Under The Veil of Pain 10

The Silent Depth 11

The Other Story 12

Tumbling Down 14

That's What Left In Us 15

You Wake Up One Day 16

Letter to a Part of My Heart 17

Motion of the Words 19

No Taglines 20

To Comfort a Throbbing Heart 21

Way Back Home 22

Precision of the Walls 23

This Continues 24

There Is a Reason 25

Autumn Romance 26

When It's All Wrong 27

I'm Yet Again On the Losers Side 28

Won't You Come Along 30

I'll Keep On Circling 31
Three Dots 32
Let's Find Peace 33
Traced Back to East 34
In a Place Where He Was All I Got 36
That Drizzling Lonely Night 37
For the Smile Which Is Long Gone 38
One Can't Reach 39
From That Moment to Lifetime 40
Will There Ever Be a Sunrise 41
Under the Veil of Pain 43
Still Aside Me 44
When There Is Something Left In Us 45
A Difference In the Arms of Care 46
We've Lost Ourselves and That's Fine 47
Give Me One More Chance 48
The Burning Rain 49
The Saturated Red 50
Unsure 51
Those Eyes 52
Remember the Thing Called Silence 53
Knight Will Come 54
Tear of the Shadow 55
Triangled 56

Fractured Letters 57
One in a Million 58
Is it Audible........ 59
The Other Side 60
For Once 61
A No to Never Return 62
The Rain Won't Stop Us Now........ 63
The Change is- Move on 64
Truth Be Told........ 65
Imprisoned Alphabet........ 67
Care No More........ 68
Alone in This Path 69
Pay Attention to the Odd 71
Once Again 72

I Don't Need This Road to Extend

I was never afeared of what awaits
at the end of this road
as long as you were by my side.
Never I was on the verge to
pay attention to those random talks
which carried by the breeze of my past.

For the life ahead,
with you being afar, in a strange tone
I do not need this road to extend,
let the end come aside, one hand away...
so I'll call it a day
once and forever, without a comeback
to pester you or the mighty friend of yours.

It's been hectic lately
to drive along the gutters
which I was never fond of.
It's getting harder and a lot breaking
to ride this way alone
even when you are here,
I can't sense a bit of it all.

Wave of My Thoughts

I swam along with the wave of thoughts
trying to find my shore,
somewhere down the depth of it all
I sensed the rhythm to not get sunk
and should I say, you were my water current,
as far as you are the sea of my everyday life
no need there exists to swim back.

I'm safe aloft the waves I'm fond of
never you will drown me down to the abyss,
for all I know, you are my shore,
every drop of ink the sea is painted with,
I'll be your sky, and let us meet at sunset
closer without actually being close.

You Never Talked to Me Then

You haven't sung,
the pearl drops never rained
You never talked to me then...
I haven't traced my fingers
onto the wet chest of yours
that bloomed within my arms.

I never blinked,
like the stars you confess
into your bluish eyes.
I never hid beneath
the warmth of your hair,
you never came to my arms,
I never hold you close to my heart.
You never talked to me then...

Under The Veil of Pain

The poem of rain falls aside,
I'm drenched in the moonlight
Aback my thoughts,
That cannot be revealed.

The pain wanders
In search of the sunrise,
It is never fond of the darkness
that now being poured upon.

The Silent Depth

The shore of hope
remained ill before
the ocean of hate(no sunrise)
Only the misspelled words wafted
the rest of it sunk.

Too strong was the current
and rowing against was of no use,
Intended it was to go with the flow.
As it felt the warmth of
the ocean cold.
The graceful memories swam
Not to surrender, but to survive.

'Need' the chosen word
wept like in a mourn
helping itself to breathe in
the colorless reflection
to let go of the pain of
losing the only remained love.

The Other Story

Alone like the unspoken measure
Of an old damaged diary
He carved for the shadow to behold
Alongside the torn pages
He once wrote off.

"i've heard the broken strings, tuning in"
The voice of silence echoed
From 7 miles apart, hill town
The rhythm to his acoustic guitar
Of reddish woods painted in regret.

Long forgotten it was
The music from his vocal chords
Muted it was, for as one note of
The written song would chase him down
Like the forest fire and drought.

Assure not the return
But the strings are tuning in,
The lyrics regained the strength to continue
The journey which was perplexed.
Is he going to drown in the
Once ever collapsed notes
Or survive the drought like waves

" you, the lyrics to my unfinished song,
The stage to my original, my first ever album,
The one and only award in need
You be my music, my end and beginning"

Tumbling Down

As of the end of road
That shows ' no entry '
She made the decision to
Step outside the regular storm
Which was just a breeze back then.

For the shared message
The color was blind
Portrayed in the middle of sunset.
Was that a wrong turn
Or a wrong disappearance...

Only the time can tell
The weather of tomorrow.
For the petrified letters
The whole idea might be
The opposite of what is right
Or simply everything was wrong.

A path without the same heartbeat
Refraining from the battle
Which was never a battle of words
But the war within the heart of hers.
A struggle to bear with the moment
A fight between her heart and brain.

That's What Left In Us

In the shadow of moonlight
Curled-up in the tendrils of affection
I stood like a pen without ink,
unmoved and all mistaken.
Will there ever arise a strike-off
to wash away the sin I'm fond of...

I wrote the poem of love like the fire within
I forgot to revisit, but it's time
Oh well, here we go again...
For the already paved ways
the bricks left cracks
to which I must be returned
and rebuild like it will never break again.

You Wake Up One Day

The fossil of the dreams
I took part in, lay at the frontier
Greeting the closed doors
With grief clouded all over it.
How to confirm the existence
When it still grumble like a dream?

How to close the eyes
When it revision the assembled art?
In those attire of azure,
The part vacillates.
All just a dream immersed
in the heart of emptiness.

Letter to a Part of My Heart

Sorry is no word to be whispered
when I'm unforgivable for my mistakes.
Sixteen years is no sententious
so does your pain,
Arriving at your mehandi
and writing his name on your palm
will wound my heart, even though
I will be wearing the armor of I'm okay
I deserve it, no apology can change it.

Reminiscences of tying knot with you
and walking around the god of blaze
wearing the cream colored kurta
when you were garnished in orange.
Still don't know why i left you
Leaving dark mare's tail upon sun rays
Neglecting each call and texts for two years...
Forgetting your face and pretended
"i don't know you" but
I haven't hated you just a bit.

For a year I've wandered
wondering why I've left you
but failure I became,
on finding the answers...

TORN

As dawn and dusk portrayed
all of your face and that gorgeous smile,
tears seemed to answer my question
that there is no going back
to wipe off the so painted part.

I'm proud of the girl you became
For as you've made the finest decision
Of tying knot with him
Who looks nothing like your past guy
As you said "he is gone... he is no more"
Right it sound for as
I won't be that guy yet again
Who hugged you tight, who never let you cry,
Who listened to you all night and
Who loved you more than life.

Motion of the Words

It was walking
alone in the roads it left
It once closed the entryways
on it's own, promising not to
take that path again.
Within that questionnaire
the answer was meant to be
the words were meant to be.

taken by the path again
Disintegrating the sentence of trust
with the differentiation
of the already printed essay
of an objective type article.

No Taglines

For all the functioning machines
there exist the brain of an expert
but for the unbroken, the still existing
chord of bonding, there lies no expertise...

Through the tornado and the tides
you remained my water current,
for all the words that left unsaid
you stood like a reader who already knew
what I wished to deliver.

Walking by your side, you made me
forget to breathe but to never get hurt.
All those unfinished poems
had your name like a watermark on it.

For the firmament, you are the sunrise
the drizzle, the never-understood comet...
Deep inside there we still write
"It's not about the time we spent together,
but about the times we crossed
and always missed each other".

To Comfort a Throbbing Heart

Behind the lockdown days
there lied an expectation
to walk towards another meet
and to hear that voice again....

What'd happen if there was
no initiative to meet and
to talk after two long spins...
"We can talk someday, there is still time.."

It's life and this headline
can be a false agreement
and time already told us this
for as there is no stories in front.

Way Back Home

As the mare's tail
summarized the whole day
with it's dark art....
the window pane of the bus
was still closed...
Restricting himself from
drenching in the rain and pain..

Unsure of the reunion
Unaware of the distant decisions...
He was stuck, somewhere between
the hardest and happiest
stories he once been into.

Precision of the Walls

He sat under the weather of unknown
as she read aloud page number 523
fourteenth line...
" Not every day, once in every
two months is enough"...
Months turned years
and the years continued.

For the forgotten
but the read lines there was no reply.
The favorite part of the notebook
hanged up the wall...
It was the replica of a lost
and found friendship...
One or two movements is the necessity
But the blocked area remains as such
in the name of a comforting zone.

This Continues

Your eyes sparkle like a million suns
That grin so sweet and irresistible
Am I dreaming in the middle of reality
I anticipate when my hand is in yours,
to hear you breathe those three words

Words are not enough to portray.
the vision that I envisage everyday
My heart, it throbs... it beats unknowingly
when we talk, the emotion flies
You wipe away the tears when I cry.

You aren't here,
you know the scale of this missing
Deep down we are sure of this bonding
Will always wear your name
once and for all

There Is a Reason

The reason he is not sure of
that awakened the hidden emotions
like the wandered art of historiography.
A difference he always noticed
on capturing his smile,
on witnessing the way of walk
the way he looks....
everything about him carries the uniqueness...
But this love was different
affectionate in it's fragrance
like the petrichor and the moon..

If there is a reason
It's searching in it's own hashtags
where there was no answer
to the question called " Why?"
there was something, like the
undiscovered part of this universe
in the circulating mind of his....
There is a reason and it repeats
there is a reason...

Autumn Romance

For the fallen leaves
and chilling drizzle
the tears sang the warmth
of finally getting understood,
never it was to expect a thing
but to deliver the care
even if that makes
no change in the
scripted walls afar.

It strongly played the part
of being cuddled up with
the unknown emotion
surrounded by the words
of missing or else missed you.
An understanding out of the blue
to hold on to the bond
which was never broken
and will always remain unbroken.

When It's All Wrong

A day, another and one more
the calendar was in no rush
but it played the fast and furious track
not sure how the four years
have left the station without
bidding a farewell to the platform.

The tides ran back
it never returned to the shore
like the once held hands refused to hold,
on whispering the breeze of love
It went wrong like the flying machine
which was intended to be the submarine

I'm Yet Again On the Losers Side

Never I thought, you'd forget
even when all of' em remembered.
These hill full of wishes won't last
for as I've waited for yours to arrive
but never came, and that day passes by...

From mid-night till the next morning
I kept the vibe alive,
thinking you will remember
this through the notification at least.
Whom I've became,
yet again on the losers side !!

Within these busiest hours,
I missed that text
still on the urge to receive one
but it will never arise.
For the faded smile,
I'm yet again on the losers side !!
Tell me you forgot,
or didn't remember it at all
either one of these would be enough
to accept as a wish from my side...

You didn't remember, you didn't forget

then I'm unsure what it is
another sunset without a gesture,
I'm long gone and all broken...
For the remained pieces,
I'm yet again on the losers side !!

Won't You Come Along

Oh the bending bow beyond the hills
won't you look this way
all through the branches
of this foggy morning?

Won't you come along,
to make the dales disappear
under the love all cloudy
to drizzle the silence
parting the arms on hold.

I'll always search for you
within the fading pain,
I'll always keep you
like the path of my tomorrows,
won't you come along?

I'll Keep On Circling

For the silence
I'm circling in and out,
there won't arise an end,
I'll keep on circling
till the end of it all.

Never the story of evening
was planned,
the moment of laugh
turned all dark,
I'll keep on circling
till the end of it all

Three Dots

It was, still is and always will
as it hides the shores together
assembled in the infinite axes
like a bridge invisible to the outsiders
extension seemed impossible.

The flipped pages shared
the written part and the to be flipped
carries the already concluded convos...
Incomplete the conclusion remained
Inconsolable the heart beats...

Let's Find Peace

The waves crashed against the rocks
looked weary on the loneliness.
As the aurora composed the entryway
into the azure of the firmament
it was still cold in the middle.

A path to walk by
without the heaviness in it,
isn't it beautiful to picturise
our own art in it?
an art only the emotion can create.

It isn't the same now
loneliness finds home, it's ashore
between the crashing waves
and under the canvas in blue...
it found peace, in nature
and it's home..... it's home.

Traced Back to East

On climbing the stairways
alongside a spectacled companion
the right turn, turned a lot
not-too-right at the sight
for as the crossed road
was standing aloof leaned
to the crossword brown art.

That walk went heavier
and pretension won at the beginning.
As the crowded highway
opened no way to the new entries
retrieval was the only option..
Strangeness measured the familiarity
for as the long four years
turned out too short at the end...

On the way back, got dragged
to the left, near the crossed road.
Pretension remained impossible
on witnessing the smile...
As the walk continued
after the knitting of a tored bond
vision was blurred.....
somewhere back in the college

stairways I've seen him
Oh stranger... you are

In a Place Where He Was All I Got

The end of story
was written all over the canvas
when the film of our journey
went all voiceless
like I've pressed the mute button,
with the initiation of
announcing the wordless word
in the most dramatic theatre of all,
the third floor balcony.

Another beginning from the end,
a decision to call of the war
when both sides were armed with AK-47
thinking only of ourselves
and not considering one another.

I can't call the end, The-End,
for as we've rebuild the collapsed wall
with hollow bricks, no hard feelings
amongst us, now it is just us....
No end is really the end, it is the beginning
of another journey, another story
which would think of it's end
but still that would be another beginning.

That Drizzling Lonely Night

She was in her soaked clothes,
examining the drizzling dark shaded sky
through that already drenched windowpane
for his arrival...

The promises seemed to get sunk
like the paper boat that was
already wet by the countless drops
of rain carried by the husky wind.

For the Smile Which Is Long Gone

It is as empty
as the barren land,
his eyes.
No vision ahead,
only the fractured memories lie.

One Can't Reach

A barrier in between us,
thickening with the cold air around.
Only a hand distance,
but this road portrayed
the endlessness, one can't reach.

Both gazing into emptiness
with pretension of I'm alright
but I'm not, unsure about the other end
We are in this endlessness
one can't reach.

From That Moment to Lifetime

For a moment
I felt the world around me
slowing itself like an old damaged clock
reaching and not reaching the exact time...

A gaze i couldn't resist,
those eyes which would tell you a story
without actually telling
"Precious, i think I'm in love"

I remember that stare
from the highschool corridors,
He turned around
and I was in love, like a ship
sailing against a desert
I didn't know how to row,
never knew how to paddle.

Amongst those pine trees
we build this home of emotions,
aback the fights and heartbreak
we moulded this bonding,
I can't let go and I won't.

Will There Ever Be a Sunrise

To all those words
that floated outside the circle
that I never thought would
come out as such from your side,
'there is a part of him that is beyond
the zonal range of jealousy and pride'.

When the emotions
didn't portray the story like
the heavy rain, I was numb...
He is the same person I've known
for more than half my life.
I can't resist but agree with your thought
" Yes, it was and is just for the money ",
for the understanding you made,
I'm no one to change it...
at the end of the day, its just you and me.

A cascade of drained smile
escaped into the sea of silence
leaving me in the fear of losing him,
the unpredictable partner in town.
Oh tell me you just want me out
from your life, I'll walk away like
there was no 'us' in between the counts,

or tell me to stay, I'll be your side till the end of it all.

When the wave of 'go away'
reaches the shore of my confusing self,
I felt the grains of sand amongst us
mending a wall in between,
Will there be a sunrise up in the hill
to look into and get bathed upon?

Under the Veil of Pain

The poem of rain falls aside,
I'm drenched in the moonlight
aback my thoughts,
that cannot be revealed.

The pain wanders
in search of the sunrise,
it is never fond of the darkness
that now being poured upon.

Still Aside Me

Impossible it is for me to resist those giggles,
as far as she is who she is,
a title of 'my girl' suit her not,
for as I'm not her guy...
All those smiles I've captured
is still here scattered in my thoughts,
wherever I go I'll carry her with me, unknowingly.

For all the steps I've taken,
there is her footprint invisibly alongside.
Like a feather in the wind, I'm falling
for the dew in her...
my breeze of happiness, she remains.

When There Is Something Left In Us

For the passed time
this story is just a memory,
but for the one ahead,
it's an emotion to live the moment
disregard of what it'll bring...

At least it is beating
like it needs another run around the corner,
for as it is not the time
to say good bye like the last moment.

A Difference In the Arms of Care

A difference in the arms of care
now loosen up to let go of a track
which was never ready for a race
but came out as such.

How to bear the burden of joy
which reflects the pain in style.
I smile with broken pieces,
A sense of thought to feel the difference.

We've Lost Ourselves and That's Fine

As the strings quoted
the note of the dwelling soul,
vagabond the never whispered
chain of words became.
Searching the miles as if
we've lost ourselves like
the diverging road, a wrong turn.

The paths came in
like the zigzagged emotions
leading the castle of bricks invisible
Here I am, aside you stand
Lost we are like the avalanche
groping for the greenery...
Aloft the painted craft of
the azure surface, we dance
with candles lit, stars they said.
we've lost ourselves and that's fine.

Give Me One More Chance

Isn't beautiful
to bow before the pain
when it's like the shining star
of your pretty face.
I desire not the love
but the affectionate sore
of a written wound
which was in terms of a song.

Forgiveness is in need
of an approval, tell me
I deserve at least an apology.
For all the words
that cleared off the surface
of a friendship zone
Forgive me for the childishness
Love me for the braveness
Hate me not for my selfishness
Forgive me for I know
whatever I did was wrong

The Burning Rain

For the collapsed words
from the melodious afternoon
of a day post to the 'mon'
there blossomed a reveal
in the hue of gloomy clouds
with no weather aside.

As it rained heavily
with rays of burning circle penetrating
through the cross-patterned window
it wasn't dark but crimson red,
there found no stop
but a full stop was necessary.

The Saturated Red

It worn the color
I couldn't remember
Was it saturated with
the love now curled up in silence.
Am afraid it's gone
the color I've known
for more than a four long turn.

As the crimson red
witnessed the glare of stare
We were only a drift apart
Tangled up in the circle
of friendly reminder...
Hear, I repeat this had seen
the best of us...
It wasn't just a color
It was us.

Unsure

Where has the wind gone,
of the times I knew.
Will it come back
like a tornado to wear
the emotionalism
I can't get rid off

Those Eyes

As he put sand upon the portray of hers
and wiped it away
it was just another try to forget the pain.
Seeing her on the dance floor
and getting congratulated by her voice

He couldn't think of anything more.
The eyes that glittered
even at the darkest night
kept coming back to him
as if she was meant to be his only love.

Remember the Thing Called Silence

As the preferred avenue
plighted the plumaged reminiscence
he had a plummet to undergo
the measurement of a riddle
for which there still reverberates
the unknown answers..

Was that a labrynth
for all the lanes he ran,
for all the lakes he swam
for all the lanterns he lit.
A latent affection
in the middle of an epitaph
embracing the invisible and invincible chain

Knight Will Come

Running up into the tower
And dreaming of a knight
who shall come with the shine of love
afar from the mountain tops

For the pedestrians I always see,
there lies the portray of
love that I always need.
My knight and his glistening sword
will it always remain a dream alone.

I lie beside the tower of hope
drenching myself in the rain of dusk
Dream, I hear the voice alone
to dream of my only knight
afar the hilltop....

Am I sure of this moon
that sails the galaxy of my home
it's dark inside but I see the light
for I'm sure my knight will come

Tear of the Shadow

As if I'm wiping off
the tears of the shadow
on the mirror facing myself,
the days of our silence lasts....
by lifting the fingers
like a roof restricting downpour

Triangled

The broken pieces still wear
the reflection of a triangular track.
It paced forth, entrapped in deviation
and traced back to the line of sight.
Why there is no getting out
from this tangential art...
Why the track tantalized
the centroid of this chart.....
Amidst this Illusion of geometry
I'm an ignorant

Fractured Letters

The plastered written notes
lost the sensation,
now knowing the not-too-painful pain
and laughing at the weeping ink
addressing the line of fate.
Will there begin a chapter
to reconstruct the fractured.

One in a Million

The wound is the cure now
to have the imprinted gale of
suffocation of the shore aloof,
she knows, hers is not broken....
The listener to the ultrasonics
even with the no-hearing bless.

Is it Audible

For the withered whispers
may there remain
an orchestrated backdoor
to never let go of this
only tune he is fond of.

The Other Side

For the blurred aurora
Sun wore the pages of pale
resembling the Moon
the aching art of affection
on the other side

For Once

Even in the reluctance
he never relinquished the fair play
Awakened in the mid night
expecting a Positive sign
once and for all.

A No to Never Return

As the finalized sentence
resembled a dot
not extending to North
but stuck within the inclined angle
the reversal track stood fixed...
Booked the train to never return
for as the dot encircled
the tangent of 'NO'

The Rain Won't Stop Us Now

Tangled up in the rays of sunshine
amidst the past and present
the drizzle portrays the art
we once painted in the egoism.
To have it in the opposite sign
alongside the impossible synonyms
is a blessing.....

Isn't it beautiful
to match each emotion as such
within the restricted lines you drawn
under the cascaded circuits.......
To wear your name
and to drench in your rain
when there was no sign
of a return........

I can be the downpour you wish for
the horizon you dance onto.
Even though I clear the zone
as the opposite side of town
I can be your home village......
Come let's find and surrender....

The Change is- Move on

For this temperory existence
there shall not be a permanent station
to wait and to recall.
Dignity may not be a disgrace
to loosen up the tightened lungs
under the splash of a journey.

Like the engine and IC
this life will rust without a test
you need to adjust.
Across the shaded Sundays
and the well assembled Fridays
there will always last a breeze
still unchanged, even within
this changing strategies.

Truth Be Told

As he walked past the corridors
adorned in blossomed lillies
music was still audible..
Words entangled in retrospection
'oh take me back to the start'
repudiated the hidden emotions....
The 523 retro track remains unchanged.
It's over, it was already...
Now the 'official' tag made the frontier.
The path seemed endless,
legs went heavy as he continued..
Nine long years..... always carried the name,
as if one day he'd wear it all by himself.

Like the snowflake of summer
destiny played the role of sunset..
witnessed the sentence of himself
like a reflection as the ring encilrcled another
where he stood like the viewer of his favourite show
A few clicks to save the moment
two or more handshakes to deliver the 'ok' synonym,
Never he had the strength to
look into his eyes, he never needed
the sympathetic look from his part
'It's all gone and you must move on'

echoed everytime he tried to recall the so-called past...

A new beginning from both sides
yet again from the cracks of a castle of glass....
Its another journey
alone in this track he walks...
alone in this phone calls he talks
alone in this messenger pad he texts
alone in this race he chases
alone in the arms he sleeps
all alone, but not willing to surrender
It's ok at times, it's not ok most of the times......
Let's not go back
let's not pace forth, stay in the present
enjoy the rest.....
Things will be alright....

Imprisoned Alphabet

'No' was the expected train
on the station of 'what about tomorrow'
for as some turns aback
he stopped booking for the same...
Never willing to be in that again

it's time to rethink,
it's time to give it a go.....
two years will hit the mark
after eighteen counts.....
Don't know of the promised noon
not sure of the words to be delivered....
Alas, clear the firmament
hope not to cloud it again.

Care No More

For the nanoscale of flight 9
and the microwave of one to twenty
emptiness fills the shadow of noon
near the broken window....
Glasses of sunrays radiates
into the other side like
contradictory to the alive present..
A reversal theory announced the rest

ignorance, egoism, and yesterdays....
How to survive if it's turning back
yet again to compress the
elasticity of this closeness.....
How to go beyond the check for text
symptoms.....
How to not bend again and
keep this attitudism....

Alone in This Path

As the aurora strolled
alone into the arms of horizon
it was ill in the branches of emptiness
and reflection were unseen....
Holding on to the heart
of the withered letters....
and tightening the lungs
with unbearable toxins....

Yesterday clanged upon the
firmament of picture perfect spring...
A dashing sunrise under his breath
sensing the loudness in that
silent field with their footsteps....
Meadow became their home
stars sung them lullaby...
it was full, clasping hands
gazing into each others eyes
exchanging the promises
through the wind......

As he walked away just like that
when the blue line offered
another close look at the sunrise,
path alone remains next to her

aurora reflects his beautiful face
within those branches
still she search that wind
with the hues of that gorgeous spring.

Pay Attention to the Odd

Not of the scars
I drew before the night
but of the time
I drowned before my eyes
this novel lasts.... tending to tear away
the following clash
the one in which I almost tried....
Try may not symphonies
the forwarding slash upon the
cheque in line....

Pay attention to the odd
not to the even play
a full stop at the unnecessary edge
a comma to continue the journey I once portrayed.....
Question mark towards the answers
Exclamation upon the unexpected....
It's time, not to survive
but to never surrender.....
Don't play the odd, play the man.

Once Again

As the iridescence of footprints
grace upon the shaded pages
of the meadow wearing
the giggles of blade of grass,
will there last a chance
to track the lane of sunshine.

To north towards the east
vesting to witness the sea
to envision the aurora sorting
the sensible blue lines.....
Once again I may not see
for as this drizzle may turn to
flood the existence of trees....
this sunrays may burn the midnight
Once again...... again and again

Notes

THANK YOU FOR READING

www.ingramcontent.com/pod-product-compliance
Lightning Source LLC
LaVergne TN
LVHW100336181026
850499LV00039B/1111
* 9 7 8 9 3 5 4 5 8 4 1 8 3 *